Poems in November

poems by

Mary Cuffe Perez

Finishing Line Press
Georgetown, Kentucky

Poems in November

Copyright © 2019 by Mary Cuffe Perez
ISBN 978-1-64662-078-4 First Edition
All rights reserved under International and Pan-American Copyright Conventions. No part of this book may be reproduced in any manner whatsoever without written permission from the publisher, except in the case of brief quotations embodied in critical articles and reviews.

Publisher: Leah Maines

Editor: Christen Kincaid

Cover Art: Ray Bilcliff

Author Photo: Kenneth Perez

Cover Design: Elizabeth Maines McCleavy

Printed in the USA on acid-free paper.
Order online: www.finishinglinepress.com
        also available on amazon.com

>Author inquiries and mail orders:
>Finishing Line Press
>P. O. Box 1626
>Georgetown, Kentucky 40324
>U. S. A.

To Kimberly

Time
caught in the act
of turning.
Hills peaked in gold,
held
in a glass globe.

You can see yourself there.

Then it rains.
For three days
it rains
leaching trees and sky,
leaving little to stay for.

You go, too.

The way you have come,
the way you have come for years now,
vaguely disillusioned,
past red-sided barns and white-sided houses,
over bridges and tannin stained streams,
past inns,
their shutters closed.

The days go blank behind you,
shorn of song and hospitalities.
If anyone passes now, they might see a man
uphill of a ragged pasture

caught
in the truth of November.

November.

Fall gone to rust.
Rust of the hay rake left in the field,
rust of the tractor sunk to its rims.
Rust of all faith
in starting over.

That's how his old man saw it,
how he sees it, head down,
minding chores.

So why this morning
did his eye catch the oak leaf drift?
Charged with light
and kidney red,
carrying something
about hanging on the longest.

He has no words for that.

Now his throat goes dry for the name
that holds the color inside the leaf of the oak.
He watches sometimes too long
their linger, let go, and spin. Equivocal
in descent.

Each
something to think about.

She could only watch
their long walk up the hill
with the sky losing light
and the oak
all that was there.

Two men,
the mare between,
head dipping to pain
each step brought.

She could only watch.
The men, the horse,
thrown in shadow.
Out again, black
against a lavender sky.

The men, the horse, the tree.
A swarm of leaves
twisting time.

Were they leading the mare away
or to her again? A filly
throwing her head.
Too much to handle.

You'll never ride her
he swore on that day.
You'll never ride her.
But she did

all the way
to now.

The sky sheds birds.
Leaves letting go
speckle the pond
and geese plow into it, their wake
pulling loose the hem
of shoreline.

Clouds gather,
rage, stomp away, storms pass
and suns and moons
settle their light upon it.

Still wide-eyed,
the pond takes everything in,
lets it sink or drift.

And ice, once again,
takes up its mending.

She is only three.
Nose running,
hat slipped over her eyes
so all you can see
are the bulbs of her cheeks
bright as the woolen coat
she wears and the apples
she hopes to catch in the basket
her arms don't quite reach around,
looking up

at you

swinging from a high branch
to shake the apples
down,
the last of the apples,
down
into the leaves, the grasses
and first fallen snow
but not in the basket

below.

And that face.
That laughing, wind-burned face.
Looking up,
looking up.

The stack of beech
cut this year
for next,
oozing sap and echoing song.

Beautiful trees
in the broken light.

Broken trees
in the beautiful light.

It was this month they began in,
an odd time for
beginnings, with winter's breath
hanging in the air
wanting to put an end to things.

Hands rough as raw boards,
he was always fixing something
come loose on the old barn,
kept a few stock and otherwise
to himself.
Words like driven nails.
Always turned away.

She liked that he could do that,

and the quizzical set of his head,
the swirl of hair at the nape of his neck
and the taper of his fingers
when he set the rail in place.

She could have walked away
that day

when he offered
to make a fire.

This is the month you choose to forget.
Wading through tides of leaves on a hillside,
the smothered song of winds.

This is the month
you fear most getting lost in.
Winter will bury you
but November trails goodbyes
unanswered.

This is the place you come to
at the edge of thickening dark,
when the low light nests
inside a grove of beech

and asks you
to lose the path. Let it grow over,
be gone. Then enter
this lair of light
made for you

or, like the deer at daybreak,
it will rise and quickly move on
leaving not a dent
of its passing.

He called them witness trees.
Hardly trees at all, she thought.
More like mastodons
caught in the mire by their roots,
bodies black as fossils, twisting in a fire.

Not witness to anything.

Boundaries, he yelled into the wind
that day they walked the woods
beyond the north pasture.
Boundaries, he repeated,
pointing to the trees.

She saw nothing but forest
in a wind pestering everything.

He showed her where the road had been,
the breaks in the stone wall
leading to the hollow of the old homestead,
shards of crockery and a cellar wall
green-backed as tidal wash.

The wind unsettled her.
The hole of a well opened up,
smelling of wound and rot
and what was buried there.

The witness trees, horrible now,
began to moan and whimper
in a voice too close.
She hurried back down the path
ahead of him

into the pasture
where the cows were, past the barn
where the chickens were,
the house was, smoke
still rising from the fire they'd lit.

He sees his mother there,
in the same light
at another window,
staring into the mist
that has stolen everything
past the apple tree.

Never taking her eyes from
the window
as if expecting a pattern
to rise,

she pulls thread through cloth,
mending the season gone to shreds,
the rooster under the dripping eaves,
the low flying geese, a seam
to stitch the sky. Things as they were
when the tractor ran.

Behind him
The sky tears itself open.
Black, purple-edged clouds
blow cold down the back of his neck.

Cows hunch over silage,
unstirred by the sky that stalks,
then devours the day left there.

He looks to the house
huddled in dusk.
Sun fades into the hill behind it
and the clutch of gray limbs
could be the hover of smoke.

He stops, looks again. No smoke
rises from the chimney.
To the north, the palest blue
is being closed in on.
Innocence caught in darkest intentions

like she was.

Would she have come to him
had she paused, looked over his shoulder
at the land he came out of?

How do the old trees give
when all that is left
is this rim of bark clutching hollow?

Apples red as ardency,
tasting of birch buds and ginger.
More this year than last.
More than she has baskets for.

Broken, twisted and towering,
the trees hold the best just out of reach,
bright as ornaments,
lit by sun.

She leaves them for the deer.
The highest for the turkeys
striding out of the hedgerow
as first light skims the frost.

One by one
they shed solemnity
and lift into the trees,
black robes fluttering and foolish
as they tip the high branches
and knock down the apples

to one who is always waiting.

November.

What hasn't left
closes up, shuts down,
leaves a few gifts by the
apple trees,
cold-burned and blighted.
The blood prick of chokeberry
in the hedgerow,
the intolerable green
of last gasp grasses

and sunflowers.
Her glorious, lofty sunflowers
always come down to this.
Heavy headed, bent old ladies
easily stolen from.

She would go without a word
wearing her black rubber boots
and his red flannel shirt
whipping like a flag behind her
as she entered the pasture
and waited.

The horse terrified him,
how it rolled its eyes and blew,
kicked up at every wild notion.
But there she stood, halter in hand
while the damn thing stomped the earth,
circled,
and threatened a storm

but always came down to her,
like there was never a doubt to it.

She'd take the trail up the north hill,
be locked off in hemlocks
until the last hold of light
slipped off the hilltop.

He'd watch out the back door for her,
seeing each time the white blaze
ripping a hole in the dark. The horse,
lathered and riderless,
headed for the barn.

But he knows better.
That horse would never come back.

Farms look strong from the road,
rooted in rock and mind.

Don't let them come inside
when they stop for syrup,
apples and pumpkins.
Don't let them see
that old crone, failure,
fumbling in the webs.

Keep talking,
smile, wave
as they go.
They'll not guess
what you keep out of sight.
As long as the barn stands true,
the roadside fences
mended.

It's all you have.
The fake front
of an ancestral farm,
listing in the wake
of the promise you made.

The woodstove sighs,
pops. Firelight
fiddles over wall and ceiling
and the drift of her body.
Shoulder to hip, so well known to him,
he could go there, stay there,
even be welcome a while.
The slope from cheekbone
to neck to collarbone,
the most
beautiful part of her.

He can enfold her completely.
She is a wound
he wants to heal,
a fox in a trap
he wants to free.

But even now
she is someplace else.
Perhaps this
is the most beautiful part of her.

Leafless,
trees lean into silence.
This is what they are here for,
not to say what the wind will have them say
but to listen for this hour
when shadows take a knife edge
and draw down their length,
slice up forest,
cross the road.

At this hour
he feels he must beg forgiveness.
For what? he shouts,
wrenching open the gate
that keeps nothing in.
For what?

Everything that is given
is taken.
It is the hardest truth to hold,
but she does now.
Grown round it
like a slash in an oak
struck by lightning
many years gone.

It is now the bend of her shoulders,
the crimp in her smile.
No small hands of sorrow
reach her here, no love
bolts from her spine.

But this month of doors blown open
brings distance stomping in
with a cold wind at its back.
Even the deer are too big
for the landscape they cross

and light,
the dagger thrust of light.

His mother came to lose things.
Needles and scissors at first,
then their names, and finally
her way.

Wandered off in a cold gray rain.
Not far,
just down by the pond.
Elderberries, she said,
when his father came to fetch her.
Something's done away with them.
Then she laughed that crumpled way
that said this is how we know life to be,
and sighed, *birds I guess.*

Not in this season
he said, steering
her back inside.

Not in November.

In this month
the hunters come,
settle like crows
among the trees, waiting
for deer to cross.

The deer cannot be found.

Stillness does not compose them
among the stand of beech.
The heat of their bodies
does not lead to
wherever it is they go.

They have slipped from their traces
through orchard, pond and pasture.

The deer cannot be found.

Wherever she looks,
hunger looks back.

That nest of the goldfinch
dangles its woven cup
from the thin fingers of
the sapling,
gone beggar now.

November hasn't coin enough
to give. Only a strong west wind
can blow away
the hope of it.

Sometimes she thinks
she has never sat in this room
or looked from this window onto
the lose tin of the chicken shed,
the pasture gone to switch grass,
and the black line of trees
holding back distance.

But she has always lived in November.
Never one for frittery or pastels,
she is suited to the core -
ocher and burnt umber,
wood and stone,
the earth bared.

And the frank want of limbs,
whatever it is
they reach for.

At first, you cannot name the silence.
All you know is the great white space of it
until a hesitant, half note
falls. A finch or jay
perhaps.

And you say, *Yes, that's it.*
Bird song.

Each note brought up from under
into green
so startling it tears
a little. A drop of red. A rose.
Streams that jump their banks.

All undone now,
leaving the sky so wide, so blank
you stop midway
between whatever it was
you were doing

as you will come one day
to stand
in the wide field of days
and say, *yes, that's it.*
Life.

The first hard frost whitens the grass,
kills off the rest of the collards,
collapses pumpkins.

His father would have thrashed him
for what he failed to bring in. This follows him
as he hauls buckets of mash to the barn,
takes stock of the loss,

and will not look
for small footsteps in the frost ahead
starting out straight enough
then swirling in pursuit

of glitter on frost,
trying to catch a wink of it,
swinging her bucket of gizzards for the barn cats,
turning back to hurry him along. Breath
white as frost.

Showing him the way.

I am the one
the squirrel forgot.

Out of a year
of heavy mast
so far back you were acorn, too,
folded inside your own long dream.

Buried deep within a squirrel's larder,
covered with loam and leaf
and two feet of snow,

I bided time.

Revolutions of light
that light recalled

a pale green hope
to climb and grab
in fists of root,
to suck and pump
and rise
to articulation
of bud and leaf,
communion with winds,
commerce with sun,

kindling
breath and song and shelter

now
warming this room
you have come to,
my last breath a whisper.
Even now I bring you life.
I, a thing
a squirrel can squander.

Like a drunk in a rage,
the storm kept up all night,
tore into the next day. Winds
rammed the old barn head on.
Rain sliced through
the ridgepole.
The maple lost a limb.

Now it's done, all that mad
thrown down
like a broken ax.
Gone off, thank God,
dragging a few wispy clouds
behind.

The sun just going down,
creeps out like
an old hound.
Beaten but back again.

Full letting-go moon.

Too steeped in earth
to move. For now
it belongs to them.

For now,
they are whole again.

But space intervenes.
Space always intervenes.

Pulling it out of the grip of limbs
and their own
ponderous need.

They must let it go.
They must let it rise.

A cold and white
heavenly body
leaving only light enough

to see the sense that
shadows make.

Geese break over the hill,
shatter the sky just feet above where she stoops,
 knees in dirt, setting bulbs.

Cold scalds her hands and her nose drips
as she fumbles to place each bulb
where it must go,
sixteen to a row, six inches apart.

Too late she answers the hungering call,
the pull to let go and go.
She bows to the earth
and gathers the count

as geese set wedge to sky.

It could be March as easily as November.
A cup half filled.
A coming not going.
One of the days you wake in,

the door ajar.

You walk from room to room
wondering whose house this is
and why nothing moves,
not dust on air
or the trees outside.
Even light stands still
and the shadows are afraid to let go.

You want to tip the cup
and spill the light
but you are held
in the stun of silence

and stillness has locked
even the hearts of small animals.

The first snow
of the season
sifts secrets through the last leaves
of the beech and oak.
It feathers the firs and hemlocks,
fills the gaps in things.

In the last days of November
you return,
expecting a change of scene.

If you pass just now
on the way to a cozy inn
blinking welcome
like a forced flower,
you might see the man and woman
walking the long road to the house
and yearn for just this:
the daily walk to the mailbox,
the keeping of animals,
smoke rising from the farmhouse chimney.

If the two had a sled
to draw behind them.
A child. And if there was a dog,
a collie, running alongside

then it would be perfect.

A scene in a glass globe.
Just what you have been looking for.

Mary Cuffe Perez, Galway, New York, is author of *Barn Stories,* a collection of non-fiction published by North Country Books, which won the 2018 award for Best Memoir from the Adirondack Writing Center; two children's books, *Gnarlys of the North Woods* (Hobblebush Press, 2019) and *Skylar,* (Penguin Books, 2008); and two collections of poetry, *Nothing by Name,* (Shaggy Dog Press, 2012); and *The Woman of Too Many Days* (Calyx Press, 2000). She has also published articles in *Adirondack Life, The Conservationist, Yankee, Northern Woodlands* and other magazines, and poems and short stories in numerous literary journals.

Mary has been awarded two artists grants from the New York State Council on the Arts for *Nothing by Name,* inspired by a Galway farm woman (2007), and *What We Keep: Life Stories from Maplewood Manor,* a booklet of memoirs from nursing home residents (2013). She created and directed Story Quilt, a social history, literary project of the Galway Public Library which won the Shubert Award for Excellence in Library Programming from the NYS Education Dept. in 2007.

www.ingramcontent.com/pod-product-compliance
Lightning Source LLC
LaVergne TN
LVHW041513070426
835507LV00012B/1532